SCIFAIKUEST
February 2024

6	A Little Help, Please
8	Editorial
12	The Chad ~cliff~ Reichard Page
13	The Jenelle Clausen Page
14	The Goren Lowie Page
15	The Guy Belleranti Page
16	The Wendy Van Camp Page
17	The David C. Kopaska-Merkel Page
18	The Stephen C. Curro Page
19	The Dan Smith Page
20	The Alejandro Barrón Page
21	The James O'Melia Page
22	The Denny Marshall Page
23	Prehistoric Hippo by Denny Marshall
24	The John Granville Page
25	The Bill Fay Page
26	Melting by Jade Foo
27	Scifaiku
33	Tanka
36	Other Minimalist Forms
44	Article: Grabbing the Snake by the Tail by Robert E. Porter
51	Featured Poet: Francis W. Alexander
61	Interview: Francis W. Alexander
63	Haiga by ARPY
64	t.santitoro: my favorite poem

THE STAFF OF SCIFAIKUEST:
TERI SANTITORO, EDITOR

SCIFAIKUEST is published quarterly online and in print. The two editions are different.

Cover art "Mars 4a" by ARPY
Cover design by Laura Givens

Vol. XXI, No. 3 February 2024

Scifaikuest [ISSN 1558-9730] is published quarterly on the 1st day of February, May, August, and November in the United States of America by Hiraeth Publishing, P.O. Box 1248, Tularosa, NM 88352. Copyright 2024 by Hiraeth Publishing. All rights revert to authors and artists upon publication. Nothing may be reproduced in whole or in part without written permission from the authors and artists. Any similarity between places and persons mentioned in the fiction or semi-fiction and real places or persons living or dead is coincidental. Writers and artists guidelines are available online at https://www.hiraethsffh.com/scifaikuest.

Guidelines are also available upon request from Hiraeth Publishing, P.O. Box 1248, Tularosa, NM, 88352, if request is accompanied by a SASE #10 envelope with a first-class US stamp. Subscriptions: $28 for one year [4 issues], $44 for two years [8 issues]. Single copies $9.00 postage paid in the United States. Subscriptions to Canada: $33 for one year, $51 for two years. Single copies $11.00 postage paid to Canada. U.S. and Canadian subscribers remit in U.S. funds. All other countries inquire about rates.

What???
No subscription to
Scifaikuest??

We can fix that . . .

https://www.hiraethsffh.com/product-page/scifaikuest-1

Or get a sample back issue to check us out!

https://www.hiraethsffh.com/shop-1

And a subscription makes a great gift, for a holiday or any time of the year!

Minimalism:
A Handbook of Minimalist Genre Poetic Forms

This handbook contains articles about how to write various minimalist poetry forms such as scifaiku, senryu, sijo, haibun, empat perkataan, ghazals, cinquain, cherita, rengays, rengu, octains, tanka, threesomes, and many more. Each article is written by an expert in that particular poetry form.

Teri Santitoro, aka sakyu, who assembled this handbook, has been the editor of Scifaikuest since 2003.

https://www.hiraethsffh.com/product-page/minimalism-a-handbook-of-minimalist-genre-poetic-forms

A Little Help, Please

In the world of the small indie press we fight a never-ending battle for attention to our work, as writers and in publishing. Here's an example: big publishers [you know who they are] have gobs of $$$ that they can devote to advertising and marketing. Here at Hiraeth Publishing, our advertising budget consists of the deposits for whatever soda bottles and aluminum cans we can find alongside the highways. Anti-littering laws make our task even more difficult . . . ☺

That's where YOU come in. YOU are our best promoter. YOU are the one who can tell others about us. Just send 'em to our website, tell them about our store. That's all. Just that.

Of course, we don't mind if you talk us up. We're pretty good, you know. We have some award-winning and award-nominated writers and artists, plus other voices well-deserving to be heard [not everyone wins awards, right?] but our publications are read-worthy nevertheless.

That number once again is:
www.hiraethsffh.com

Friend us on Facebook at Hiraeth Publishing

Follow us on Twitter at @HiraethPublish1

SALE!!

There's a sale going on!! It's still going on!!

All the books you can order at 20% off the total! Woot!

Buy 1 book; buy 100 books! It's all the same discount. Use the code **BOOKS2024** when you check out.

Go to the Shop at www.hiraethsffh.com and make those selections now!

You'll be glad you did. So will we.

EDITORIAL

Greetings, Readers!

Happy New Year, and Happy Valentine's Day!

Time really speeds by, doesn't it? Already we're into the second month of 2024. Here's hoping that this will be a really wonderful year full of love. We need one. Between Covid and the war with Hamas, the Earth and its people have been struck some horrible blows recently. When are we as a species going to learn to live together in peace? To live and let live? To respect each other? What we do to ourselves now cannot help but affect the future of our planet. When do we draw the line and say, Enough is Enough? Time races by and, instead of becoming more enlightened, we seem to be devolving, to our own detriment. Maybe we need a really fantastic year to change our outlook. Instead of gloom and doom, perhaps we need some miracles. Hate to tell all y'all, but those miracles are up to US.

Scifaikuest **now has its own ISBN!!! Please inform your local bookstores and library that they are now able to ORDER SCIFAIKUEST!!!**

You can now find us at Hiraeth Books at:
https://www.hiraethsffh.com/home-1

If you don't have a subscription to our PRINT edition, they are available at:
https://www.hiraethsffh.com/product-page/scifaikuest

And, if you would like to join the select group of contributors by submitting your poetry, artwork or article, you can find our guidelines at: https://www.hiraethsffh.com/scifaikuest

You can also read our ONLINE VERSION at: https://www.hiraethsffh.com/scifaikuest-online

Pssst! Looking for something good to read?

You can get t.santitoro's newest novella, Those Who Die, at: THOSE WHO DIE by t. santitoro | Hiraeth Publishing (hiraethsffh.com)

You can also order **t.santitoro's** latest novella, *Adopted Child*, at: https://www.hiraethsffh.com/product-page/adopted-child-by-t-santitoro

You can also get a copy of her novelette, *The Legend of Trey Valentine*, at: https://www.hiraethsffh.com/product-page/legend-of-trey-valentine-by-teri-santitoro

NEWBIES: **David Arroyo, Jerome Berglund , Jenelle Clausen , Bill Fay, Goran Lowie, Keith Massey, James O'Melia, Maria S. Picone, Chris Reichard, Andrea Weiskopf** and **A. Zaykova.**

Cupid's arrows
the enemy does a complete
one-eighty

-sakyu-

Aliens, Magic, and Monsters
By Lauren McBride

Fun to read. Fun to write. *Aliens, Magic, and Monsters* features poems set in the unlimited and imaginative realm of science fiction, fantasy, and horror. The poems were chosen to showcase over twenty poetic forms from acrostiku to zip, from strict rhyme to free verse, and much more in between. There are guidelines included on how to write each type of poem. Try a sci(na)ku. At only six words, it's sure to interest even the youngest readers.

Type: Juvenile and Young Adult Poetry Manual

Ordering links:
Print: https://www.hiraethsffh.com/product-page/aliens-magic-and-monsters-by-lauren-mcbride

ePub: https://www.hiraethsffh.com/product-page/aliens-magic-and-monsters-by-lauren-mcbride-2

PDF: https://www.hiraethsffh.com/product-page/aliens-magic-and-monsters-by-lauren-mcbride-1

The Chad~cliff~Reichard Page

April Showers

tsomething about the rain
blood-soaked battle fields
bathed new

This Town Ain't Big Enough

Four rode in
scaring Angels and Demons
blazing winds of change

Glimmer of Hope

horsemen pulling Hell's reigns
as the moon sways the ocean
rising of the tide

The Jenelle Clausen Page

prehensile tree roots
needing nourishment
sleeping vagrants pulled in

midday hurricanes
the wealthy undisturbed
robot-boarded windows

human planetfall
survival advice
lie still as death

The Goran Lowie Page

unsheathed swords
the victor and the vanquished
killed the summer light

she opens her eyes
singing trees and blossoming birds
quiver on green Mars

dragon in winter
breathing swirling fog
never expected me

The Guy Belleranti Page

    my black hole escape
    can wait
    lost love found

    trail of rusty tears
    end of the line
    for robot romance

    Valentine's Day
    alien surgeon repairs
    broken hearts

The Wendy Van Camp Page

through rainbow hues
we lift off and pass Luna
einstein-rosen bridge

within gas giants
as only the south wind moves
the aeronauts flight

seeking afterglow
thin air outside Martian domes
firework rockets

The David C. Kopaska-Merkel Page

genship gardening
telling tales of suns and fields
to shoots in a cup

plutonian strip tease
down to ice
already

house of mirrors
constantly reminded
you're not the fairest

The Stephen C. Curro Page

spelunking on Mars
lanterns illuminate
blood-red tunnels

generation ship Olympics
gymnasts perform under
a star-studded dome

downtown Tycho
the stars shine
day and night

day one of terraforming
easing an apple seed
into alien soil

The Dan Smith Page

world building-
ant-like bots
toil unceasing

supernova radiation-
ship's detectors
still twinkle

deep space-
your essence
my constant warmth

The Alejandro Barrón Page

nuclear submarine
fighting against the kraken
inside a soup bowl

spaceship carefully
landing over the sand grain's
surface.

crew is ready
submarine starts to inmerse
inside the cup of tea.

The James O'Melia Page

  hitching a ride on this
     rolling rock around the sun
         aliens invade

  while I yet live on
     this green world filled with green men
         I yearn for yesterday

  handsome three-eyed man
        direct from Venus serving
        at diner nearby

     unbeknownst to her
        mere mirrors are my portals
        back to the mortals

The Denny E. Marshall Page

not the only one
who has trouble with neighbor
departing UFO

stone size meteorites
deliverer more viruses
alien presents

your release date
second of July deportation
back to planet earth

Prehistoric Hippo
Denny Marshall

The John Granville Page

replacement bureau

ambushed when I got home
my wife's lipstick
on a killbot

close shave

her laser beam eyes
remove more than stubble
flesh melting off

stasis

in punch-card stacks
world's first AI
with nothing to run on

meme

on slips of paper
a weaponized meme
readers minds gerbil-wheeling now

The Bill Fay Page

county fair
a juggler proves
the uncertainty principle

me and my first wife
more a mixture
not a compound

Schrödinger's theorem
if you swiffer a floor
a cat will appear

business conference
the true meaning
of inert gas

Melting
JadeFoo

SCIFAIKU

blinking light on a skip—
a ghost watches over
his living self's stuff

Harris Coverley

a conscious mind—
caught in a flicker of want
then his battery died

Harris Coverley

"Pet People"
Matthew Wilson

tsunami kills 3000
hands descend from sky
god rearranging his fish tank

"Witch with a Dark Heart"
Matthew Wilson

giving the new schoolgirl valentine's candy
the first gift she ever received from a boy
the first from her to cure his cancer

aliens among us
only southside Chicago
on pizza night

    Randall Andrews

spicing things up
interstellar dating app
your planet or mine?

    Randall Andrews

wind and ice greeting
cryo-fatigued colonists
awake to explore

    Maria S. Picone

3gs

the countdown begins
a giant stands on my chest
as I chase the stars

    A. Zaykova

hidden from earth's view
drones sift lunar regolith
mining the dark side

    Greg Fewer

the heart wants
what the heart wants...
brains

    Jerome Berglund

chill rain on my face
a new moon
next to the old

    Christina Nordlander

library between
two pages of time
aliens book sign

    Todd Hanks

archway
first step
to another time

    Roxanne Barbour

red blood
on the operating table
gradually turning green

    Roxanne Barbour

starship crew all dead
lonesome AI learning how
to play solitaire

    Gabriel Smithwilson

transported

matter transmitter
traveling a beam of light
natives see angels

    Herb Kauderer

getting over
my alien abduction
the aliens

LeRoy Gorman

Mars solstice
a supply ship's freight
fills with light

LeRoy Gorman

alien gunman
quickdraw with extra arms
Weird West hero

DJ Tyrer

in our deep embrace
two tongues probe me from her mouth
I love her species

Keith Massey

ocean planet blues
finding that mermaids reproduce
asexually

    Gabriel Smithwilson

Pacific 231

on the space elevator
when it snaps
your whiplash making waves

    Benjamin Whitney Norris

silver claws emerge
full moon rises on a howl
eager for the hunt

    Maria S. Picone

femme fatale's kiss
his final sensation
succubus revealed

    DJ Tyrer

visibly struggling,
the body in the bag
in the spiderweb

    Michael Nickels-Wisdom

booming summer crops
sickles and scythes in rusty shed
anointed with blood

    Daniel R. Robichaud

dusk at the playground
murmuring spectral voices
pleading for release

    Daniel R. Robichaud

TANKA

Flying Deutschmann

the U-boat adrift
out of diesel
in the Mid-Atlantic
jerry-rigged to catch the wind
with sails of human skin

    Benjamin Whitney Norris

Takeout

only protein I've had
in a fortnight...
blood on the chopsticks,
picking maggots
out of my leg

Benjamin Whitney Norris

one hundred ships
leaving their harbour
to find unseen shores
sailing not beneath the guide stars
but towards them

A. Zaykova

glass shatters
shuffles and moans
they are inside
but my wheelchair's turned over
I can't escape

Greg Fewer

born again
red leather strip club
bar stool
a life of clean living
rewarded in the next

David C. Kopaska-Merkel

I've traveled pastward
one way Cretaceous journey
my eyes surprised see
hadrosaurus squinting at
radiant comet death of us

    Keith Massey

ufo hunter
finally finds a saucer
not the way he planned
from the spacecrafts round window
sees planet earth get smaller

    Denny E. Marshall

weathering the storm

she holds together
the broken asteroid shield
long enough to live
but not long enough to land
sentenced to life in orbit

    Herb Kauderer

OTHER FORMS
(including: Sijo, Fibonacci, Cinquain, Minutes, Diminuendo, Ghazals, Threesomes, Brick, etc.)

FIBONACCI

does
life
exist,
he wonders,
on the blue and green
distant planet he watches turn
within a hazy barred spiral galaxy of light.
He longed to unearth proof of a
common universe -
no longer
alone
in
space.

Andrea Weiskopf

SATURNE

Nannybott Applicant

my
rubber
soft-soled feet
won't spoil baby's
sleep

Lauren McBride

ACROSTIKU

in the slushy layer
camera-laden water-testing robots
eyes on Europa

    Lauren McBride

SCI(NA)KU TANKA

for the aliens
with tiny
ears
must remember
to speak up

    Lauren McBride

CHERITA

Mirrored Universe

in equality

in the speed of time
lonely earth-ship in dark space

forgets all of charted law
one-woman ruler
a harem of men

    Juan M. Perez

The Dating Scene

deep meditation

sleep medication
nothing will erase sharp pain

interspecies relations
not as you recalled
far-space intercourse

Juan M. Perez

HAIBUN

Prisoner
Guy Belleranti

    The room stinks.
    Wish I could escape, but I cannot move. I can only see and hear.
    I see the door swing open, and I hear footsteps.
    The face has returned. Once again it fixes that stare on me. "The public wants to meet you," it says.
    I don't reply because I cannot speak. I cannot make any sounds. I wish I could because I want to scream.
    The face moves closer, still staring. Then I'm lifted high...

> more staring faces
> I stare back
> from my bodiless living head

Trapped!
Greg Fewer

A breeze carries trash down the empty street. John pants heavily, a groaning and shuffling mass of zombies following him. Rounding a bend, he stops abruptly, another horde feeding ahead of him.

Seeking to escape, John pries off a sewer hole cover and climbs down the ladder beneath. Flashlight out, he heads down the sewer, clear water washing his feet.

Hearing bodies splash heavily down the sewer hole behind him, he picks up his pace.

Turning at a junction, he runs into undead sanitation workers who grab and smash him against the sewer wall, their jagged teeth ripping his flesh.

> week-long rain
> Scott stops searching
> for Annie's Daddy

Haibun
William Landis

I'm not an animal person, or a people person for that matter. The constant purrs and hisses of the stray cats agitated me. But they weren't going anywhere, so I was forced to learn to enjoy their presence. Now I enjoy playing with them. See there's more than one way to skin a cat.

> I found that I
> enjoy doing it while the
> cat is still alive

a white one by the bay
Jerome Berglund

The customers kept calling in tears. With headset strapped firmly in place, rhythmically squeezing and releasing a stress ball, fingers racing across his nine-key surrounded by scented candles and aromatherapy oils, heart palpitating with gratis coffees he may as well administer directly to bloodstream via i.v. drip., the operator strove to discern the root cause of their grievances. Those machines they'd paid so much for, which were supposed to heal them, refresh them, relax them: they were not working as advertised, rather consistently injured and agitated consumers, in seemingly more new and inventive fashions each day. Bones were snapped, eyes gouged out, spines twisted or altogether snapped like brittle tree branches. Fingers were chewed off by the joint, kneecaps shattered, eyelashes singed off, organs prolapsed. First degree burns, scarring, lacerations covered bodies from head to toe. And all this service person might accomplish in his tiny office, enclosed with blank walls and stacks of manuals, was struggle to maintain his sanity, stay calm, keep his wits about him and patiently coax the callers into each admitting fault, taking personal responsibility for every injury through different citable misadventures, document the company's total lack of liability in certain terms, the customer's utter absence of any case against them or legal cause for griping, that clearly specified duties and upkeep requirements had been overtly violated – user error, negligent maintenance, failure to adhere to routine cleaning schedule, meet prescribed servicing demands as obligated by terms of service, employed off-brand replacement parts which directly violated any binding contracts, as could be reviewed, clearly stated in microscopic bolded print with hyperbolic urgency in bulletproof legalese throughout numerous disclaimers – voiding relevant warranties and waiving any claims they might have for compensatory reimbursement, remuneration for exorbitant, continually mounting medical expenses incurred as a result of operating their deadly and injurious product line. If the support person was unable to definitively establish these truths to a tee beyond a reasonable doubt he was obliged to disavow association with that discontinued fleet of devices and refer the complainant to the original manufacturers for pursuing any further communications and damages they may be due. He left the onus of securing a mandarin translator, contacting them in writing and getting said missive hand-delivered there through the countless perilous jungle passes required to reach whatever distant village prefecture the plant resided in, to their capable machinations, shredded all evidence of direct contact, dubious internal discussion surrounding the matter, purged every digital record of the ticket from their databases in anticipation of the next unscheduled audit from relevant regulatory agencies. Depending upon the volume of actionable criminal negligence, consequent maimings and incidences of preventable fatality, those inspectors would assess the reasonable bribe expected for their business to remain open and in good standing, and haggle upon the precise number until a mutually agreeable compromise could be reached and bargain struck, they met in the middle and parted ways satisfied as happiest of campers.

        day the earth stood still
        rock and roll fantasy
        camp

I Cannot Escape My Family
David Arroyo

I wake in fright. Mother stabs me. I wake in fright. Father stabs me. I wake in fright. Sister. Sinister. Twister. I wake in fright. Mother stabs me. I wake in fright. Father stabs me. I wake in fright. Sister. Sinister. Twister.

> atoms split
> the mare cleaves
> family into fetish into fiends

My First Sleep Paralysis Attack As An FSU Seminole In 2003
David Arroyo

Nazi Concentration Camps. Mr. Death. Schindler's List. Life is Beautiful. Apt Pupil. Eichman. So much Eichman. Arndt. Even more Arndt. "Did Six Million Really die?" (Yes!) Or was it just tuberculosis? (No!) To Be or Not To Be. Either way, heil myself. Heil this campus and the red-faced homecoming on Greek Row. Heil the frat-boy tee, that counterfeit coin inscribed on both sides with its truth. Heads: I Support The War In Iraq. Tails: Shoot'em All And Let God Sort Them Out.

> dark thuds step to the foot
> drags me to dachau
> can't cry for heil

When It Rules Your Nights
David Arroyo

I am forsaken by all felines. Kittens hiss. Tabbies spit. Persians bitch. Calicos won't go anywhere near me. Black cats will choke on their own bad luck before crossing my street.

> damned by the dog
> my chest its pale throne
> no best friend

Ex-Catholic and Nowhere To Turn
David Arroyo

Water. Wine. Blood. Body. Bread — unleavened bread. Solace? No Solace. Instead. Dread. Fourteen stations surround my bed. Bible at my stead. Paschal candle to handle the vandal savaging my lonely nights. Do not ask how low I've fallen. Do not ask how a former altar boy disgusted by religion acquired these sacramentals. I've gone mental indeed. Drink and eat christ before bed. Say ten Hail Marys but all I think about is Larry, the unluckiest altar boy. Rest on my side staring at the Easter nite-light. It waxes. I wane.

> the candle smiles
> wax worm wiggling
> leach of faith

Space Junk Stinks Sweet As Skunk Going Clink Clunk Kerplunk Space Junk
Denise Noe

Assigned to clean up a considerable amount of space junk, Second Lieutenant Colonel Katarina Alvarez Klunk oversees the return to earth of a bright glittering silver massive no longer used satellite that is orbiting pointlessly and giving back no information. Second Lieutenant Colonel Katarina Alvarez Klunk makes the signal and the taking up space for no good reason satellite is damaged oh so beautifully damaged and it hurtles back to the earth and enters earth's atmosphere where it explodes like a miniature supernova sizzling stunning super hues of red and yellow and blue and purple before dissolving blackly into ashes.

>space junk
>sizzling fireworks
>gone in an instant

Stranger Any Moment
Michael Nickels-Wisdom

At a certain point in summer, the corn overtakes everything around it. Tall growth on each side of the road, making an irreversible passage. And if it's planted in the right direction, you'll see those spaces between the rows, like side entries. And that effect heightens when darkness falls. You drive along. You ask yourself what might come out of one of those places, stepping onto the shoulder of the road, crossing it in two or three steps and disappearing into the corresponding opposite, with only a brief glance at you as you sit there in your car with the headlights on and the windows down and your heart racing. And you ask yourself, Did it really move like a cartoon character? What kind of thing in real life moves that way? It doesn't even need to happen, to make you uncomfortable. If it's just a coyote or a raccoon, or your mind decides in a split-second that it's a coyote or a raccoon, you're primed for that feeling anyway. And worse, if your mind, against your will, decides it's not a coyote or raccoon, then you have to keep that bottled up because no one would believe you.

> motel corridor,
> no second person around
> for Doors of Your Mind

Home Far From Home
Captain's entry: Logbook of the Starship Horizon, Stardate - 5:6:2147
Rick Jackofsky

Fifty years after leaving Europa, our dreadnaught class starship, The Horizon, enters a new solar system and shifts out of hyperspace. The move automatically activates our life support systems, taking us out of cryonic suspension. In the ensuing hours, the decks of the ship come alive as we undertake the last leg of our journey to Quintu, the fifth of a dozen planets that orbit a pair of red dwarf stars in the Niven Sector of the Gamma Quadrant.

It has taken us a few months to acclimate to the

gravitational force of our new home, which is 1.2 times the strength of Earth's gravitational pull, and it will be several more months before we have all our habitats up and running. But it's now clear that we will succeed in establishing a self-sufficient colony on our new home planet.

There's still a lot of work to be done, but it looks like we're going to be OK. It will be another decade before our strongest telescopes will be able to look back and detect the signature of our ship hurtling through space towards a destination that we have already arrived at. I wonder what it will be like for our children, and our grandchildren, to suddenly see The Horizon appear at the edge of this solar system we now call home?

> looking back
> I see myself coming
> the speed of light

ARTICLE

Grabbing the Snake by the Tail
Robert E. Porter

People like John Prine or Fred Rogers wrote songs with lyrics that stick in my head like one of John Henry's railroad spikes; I remember *them*. I've forgotten almost everything else, including most of what I've ever heard, seen, read, or written. I'm sure most readers have, too. The real poets, I think, are like West African griots, who shape their words and lines so they'll be remembered for generations – without ever needing to be written down.

Not that I don't value wordplay for its own sake. It's fun! I delight in puns, hairpin turns of phrase, plot Twister games with tangled limbs and chainsaw cut-scenes...

The horror genre that we all know and love is a literary roller coaster with built-in safety measures regardless of engineer or year of construction. Drop a library on your congressman, and he'll need more than a couple of aspirin to make the next committee hearing. But read some horror fiction and poems, or play your favorite black metal albums, and you might... upset the congressman's wife. She'll come after you with a Puritan's self-righteous fury and a Parental Advisory label. Does she honestly believe that language and imagination pose some real danger to red-blooded Americans?

YES!

To say otherwise might dispel her enchantment with verse -- and vice-versa! So, let us keep her in the dark and pretending that words are indeed magical.

As the griots and Homer knew, it bears repeating: poetry is what makes language (and its malcontents) memorable. It carries more of human experience forward than a cheap paperback thriller or Roger Corman drive-in movie. Poetry's older than civilization, older than the invention of writing; it is the glue that holds a culture together, how it learns to define (and redefine) itself.

A poem on the page is not in its natural habitat. The taxidermist's jackalope can hardly compete for mates or Metamucil with a "live" Hare Krishna, Bugs Bunny, or Eddie Rabbit.

What is a poem, anyway?

Good question!

The diversity of definitions defy description. It's fun to give it a try, anyway. For ex., defining a poem by line and syllable count. Easy, right? But...

Imagine, in response to your 5-7-5 ku:

"Your count's off."

"He's always been off."

"No, your *syllable* count."

"What?"

"Your 'i' in 'fire' is a diphthong."

"Thank God! I thought it was hemorrhoids!"

No, the "i" is virtually pronounced twice, by many people, so that "fire" rhymes with "higher" and seems to have two syllables, not one.

Lemmy Kilmister of Mötorhead was a fan of the umlaut. He put those double dots (diphthong here?) over the first "o" in the name of his band because he thought it looked mean. German, he meant? The guy hated Nazis and everything they stood for. But he liked their uniforms, daggers, and accoutrement. They had *style*. That Göring (umlaut again), for ex. From the way he changed attire, or brachiated from one guerrilla fashion statement to the next, better to compare him to Liberace or Elton John than some arch-conservative like Mao-jacketed Mao or olive drab fatigued Castro. Can't you see Göring on Late Night in rhinestone sunglasses? Playing before a "live" studio audience – and knocking them dead? *Killing* them?

That Herman Göring! He was such a ham! What a boar, that Göring was! Just horrible! Always whoring for his Fuhrer's hoary zombie hoards!

The horror genre, however, is not a swan dive off the observation deck. It is not looking for land mines with a pen light and a trowel on a moonless night in Helmand province. Compared with true horror, the genre is a Trekkie Trek biker in plumber's pants, up the road ahead, trying desperately to make it home in time for reheated bean burrito leftovers and a *Next Generation* rerun. It is a distraction, really, something to focus on – other than a broken marriage, parental alienation, a stack of unpaid bills, a traffic jam... or peanut butter allergy.

In other words, the horror genre is a relief (to be set in relief) from the real little horrors most of us face, and the big stuff (saved from global warming – by nuclear holocaust?) we try not to think about. And what a relief!

I had this from a long-time correspondent:

"We've had about two weeks of rain. Everything around here smells like mold. YUCK. Running the dehumidifier helps a bit, but still."

Which I rearranged into a loosely-goosey tanka:

> two weeks of rain.
> Running the dehumidifier
> helps a bit, but still.
> Everything around here
> smells like mold. YUCK.

The gross-out being the lowest form of horror, according to King Stephen. But it was still worth a shot, or navel broadside, even for HMS. Better than shooting blanks! Or Göring unnoticed!

When you dig that bamboo shoot down under the fungal nailbed, pry it up and look a little deeper. You'll see it too, I think. All this yucky horror genre stuff! It doesn't matter if Shaun's sheepish zombie stands in for your own dead-end job, or that cigar-shaped rocket ship is a red-eyed escapist's vehicle – or Hugo's priapic ideal. These things aren't real!

Distractions!

That's all they are. But... I wonder...

Can they keep us from climbing the walls and chewing on the light fixtures? Can they recharge us? Bring us back to earth Eveready to deal with things as they are? I don't know. Maybe. It Depends. Can they get us out of the house, anyway? Out of our heads, and into the moment? For a moment?

Do they get to the point? You know, that "aha!" moment?

The good ones do! We can read them and weep, sure -- or we can read them *out loud* and grab the plumber's snake by the tail. Give it a good hard, snap and unclog our toilet bowl minds! A royal flush! Once the turds go swirling down, the water turns clear again. We can relax and think more clearly again. But, please, for God's sake, set a different bowl out for the dog.

FEATURED POET:
Francis Wesley Alexander

The seven-time Rhysling nominee and three-time Dwarf Stars nominee is the author of *When the Mushrooms Come*, and *I Reckon*. He is a coeditor with Theresa Santitoro of the Drabbun Anthology. Recently, he has been published in *Scifaikuest, Tales from the Moonlit Path, Valley Voices,* and *Cattails*.

    sudden breeze –
    that necklace bearing
    his friend's shrunken head

    Curse of Cain –
    the crime victim remembers
    his deaths in six past lives

    surgery –
    realizing that this
    is an alien abduction

    flickering ghost –
    the pulsar
    above our heads

    gun pigs –
    gathering at the convention
    like witches at a black mass

The Doomsday Paradox (a drabbun)

Mighty phalluses packing payloads of power. A round silvery object, a UFO, hovers over the silos and momentarily makes the missiles impotent. The government spokesman speaks of investigations because something is in the country's airspace and is "a threat to the nation." The government now calls these objects "UAPs". To me, the threat is of nuclear war that we can do something about and not UFOs that make our armed forces helpless.

We fear nuclear war. We're afraid of annihilation. We're afraid we can't help it. We're afraid UAPs can.

> a cloud puff emerges
> from the larger one:
> marvelous day

Hardheaded (haibun)

Taz was a hardheaded man. If you told the short muscular man to go left, he would head right. When a person said "no", Taz would make it out to be "yes". No girl is crazy about a hardheaded man, yet, Taz couldn't figure out why he was perpetually single. We tried to help him.

I remember that fateful day when the zombies came. We were eating in Rex's Diner. Taz was harassing the waitresses as usual, and we happened to be discussing the difference between vampires and zombies. I don't know who told him that garlic stopped zombies but when Mike the Rocket Linx shambled in and bounced on the man at the table next to us, Don and I took off.

Chest out, Taz stood his ground.

"That's not a vampire, Tazman," I shouted when I saw him holding the bottle of garlic powder.

Every day, Taz knocks on my door. Day and night, he appears. "Open he ha nup, man," Taz gabbles.

> never ending apocalypse
> cannibalizing
> the zombie's thighs

Forbidden Haibun: *Worst Case Scenario*

> Cygnus:
> earth's woes cry in unison
> to the universe

Summer-like: seeds of civil war spreading across the mighty nation. Midsummer rain: the cities and towns engulfed in flames. Professional baseball has been cancelled: smoldering.

> Andromeda:
> wishing for
> the good old days

Lantern: seeing evil in every shadow. Scarecrow: enemy agents plotting and scheming. Solar storm smashing plans of surprise nuclear attack: morning cold.

> Orion:
> only auroras are spotted
> below the ISS

Tea flowers: as the firewood pops survivors offer thanks. Winter night: news that volcanos erupted from Iceland months ago. Hope that mankind has finally learned from its mistakes: withered lotus

> Cassiopeia:
> the coup de grace
> of a worldwide drought

King (a drabbun)

With his head held high and chest expanded, the king basked in the noonday sun. This would be a great victory. From the hill, he looked disdainfully at the ant-sized figures below. He squeezed his right hand as if crushing the bugs.

> scorching heat –
> being highlighted by
> the sudden burst of light

"Where am I?" the ruler asked. An icy breeze combed his skin from head to toe when he saw the beings with peach-shaped heads and black oval eyes staring at him. He was too paralyzed to cover his nakedness.

the loud hiss of a deflated balloon - sudden eclipse

Infinite Recurring Song (a drabbun)

The universe mirrors its concept of predatory behavior. Shrimp dines on plankton that ends up being eaten by other animals. The Spanish subdued the Aztecs, a mighty nation that had conquered the Tepanec. Someday, the earth will be swallowed by the sun, which will eventually be slurped by a black hole. In the future, the once vibrant universe shall crunch itself and be absorbed by the darkness. Not long afterward, the darkness will be buried by the light of a big bang and the process starts all over again.

> right on schedule
> the groundhog dining in my garden
> at dawn

Untitled (a Simon Sijo)

Walking down these steps
determined to reach bottom,
recognition wallops me
making me see stars and the winding path
extending through the gleaming rainbow light.
The consternation
that my body is shrinking
as I move down this infinite fractal.

Post Witch Trial (a Simon Sijo)

Wearing the red robe
signifying his power
as the so-called witch kneels down.
No one would believe that she rebuffed him
the priest whose lusts burned hot in his loins.
From the dark tunnel,
he drops into roaring flames
his loins bathed in fiery brimstone.

Unexpected (a Simon Sijo)

Consternation rules
due to the enemy siege
with its dreaded arsenal.
The opposing leader plans
to blot out their existence.
Sudden solar storm,
why are you changing the odds,
a requiem converted to songs of joy?

The Unjustly Accused (a Simon Sijo)

Wearing the blue shawl
a sign of his loyalty
as the king's circle applauds.
They are filthy rats who shuffle and jive
competing fiercely for the king's favor
In the dim dungeon
the chained man wondering why
his beloved king believes in their lies.

Balloon Head

Pickwick didn't mind
them calling him "Balloon Head."
And he warned everyone
that he wasn't to be a Sleeping Beauty.
Temptation is like a sneeze
that must erupt.
I saw Jake stick Pickwick's head
with a needle
An explosion of stars
like candy from a pinata.
I was in the door when it happened.
Now all I see is darkness
and I continuously hear
their pre-explosion voices

First Horror Training

It was a big bang of primal fear with symbols and images this toddler could not understand. I now know them to be night terrors, sleep paralysis, and nightmares, but at that time all I knew was that I didn't want to go back to sleep. I felt more comfortable with those voices, especially Mom's cooing, close to me.

> Cassiopeia --
> horrors and terrors twinkling
> in the night sky

Nightmares didn't care that I had recently learned how to walk. My parents, Auntie Lou, and that stranger were impressed by my feats. But when darkness came, the incubus knew I couldn't use my legs to escape it. And although the candy man and sandman seemed to conspire against me, I could not resist eating sweets before bedtime, which gave the incubus free admission to my dreams.

> Ursa Major --
> wondering if that house
> is haunted

Bullies were the creepy crawly beings I encountered in those brightly lit rooms on my journey to adulthood. Even they took second place to the evils leaping from the pages on the school shelves. Hansel and Gretel, Cinderella, and Sleeping Beauty refused to keep me company as I fretted seeing the witch's warty face and scarlet eyes seeking to find me under the covers and quilt.

> Draco --
> beginning to hide
> from the light

Frank Sinatra "It was a very good year" 17
Television hosts Ghoulardi, Sir Graves Ghastly, Dr. Shock, Svengoolie, and Vampira were some of the many hosts that made watching horror films on Friday nights fun. Sometimes I went with Gery Horn and friends to the movie theater and enjoyed the thrills and chills of the characters running from Frankenstein, the Tingler, and the Mummy. One November night while walking from the theater, we boys sprinted under the viaducts before the train arrived with its demons carrying lanterns that we heard could entrap us for eternity.

> Autumn of the year --
> a spiderweb filled
> with failed nightmares

Forbidden Haibun: *We Return*

> Centaurus:
> seeing that constellation
> for the first time

Spring dawn: imagining the view of our ship's rise to the heavens. Docking at the starship: relief that there were no accidents. Banquet: meeting our shipmates and partners for the first time. Heavenly feeling: our ship takes off for Proxima Centauri. Ninety-eight strong: each of us prepares to do our jobs.

> Southern Cross:
> a diet of Saturn, Uranus
> and Pluto

All systems go: we enter the sleep chambers and AI takes over. Light speed: through bow shock, plasma and out of the system. Sweet dreams: daily living in an alternative world. A day in the life: conflict erased with the wave of my hand.

> Little Dipper:
> awakened after nearly four years
> of travel

Proxima Centauri B: building a temporary settlement. Med check: we all have cancer and lots of mutations. All work and no play: Mai will have my first child. Mutants: witnessing abilities we never had on Earth.

> Big Dipper:
> leaving behind the dead
> and some colonists

Light speed: Earth is a welcome sight as viewed from near Mars. Stunned: my nephew looks much younger than me on the viewscreen. Dread: wondering if they'll accept my son's alien appearance.

> our return:
> feeling like monsters
> in a science fiction movie

When the Mushrooms Come
By Francis W. Alexander

The Atomic Age brought with it many wonders and great strides forward. It also brought nuclear war. We often forget how many nuclear warheads are still scattered about our world, and how many countries are still trying to make their own. What would happen to ordinary people if one fell without warning?

https://www.hiraethsffh.com/product-page/when-the-mushrooms-come-by-francis-w-alexander

INTERVIEW WITH FEATURED POET:
Francis Wesley Alexander

How long have you been writing poetry?
I have been writing poetry for a long time. I was shy as a child and sometimes I wrote poems for guys who liked the same girl I did. Writing poems for my competition allowed my poems to get to the girl since I was afraid to write one and give it directly to her. In high school, I started writing social protest poetry and had one poem in the high school showcase which was published in the city paper in an article about the first Negro History Week at our school. It wasn't until the nineteen nineties that I started getting published in magazines.

Do you write poetry other than genre poetry? If so, what kind?
Yes. Besides science fiction and horror, I write religious poems, elegies, free verse, haibun, haiku, and other types of poems.

Who is your favorite poet?
I do not have one favorite. Besides Edgar Allen Poe, Lenard D. Moore, and Langston Hughes, I also like Samuel Taylor Coleridge, Nikki Giovanni, and Lewis Carroll. My recent favorites are Marge Simon, Linda Addison, Deborah P Kolodji, Christina Sng, Terrie Leigh Relf, Lauren McBride, Kendall Evans, Lee Clark Zumpe, and Assu.

What/who is your main inspiration?
World events inspire me to write the poems I do. Also, I watch YouTube videos for inspiration. As for who inspires me? Seeing people I know who succeed at things or at least put in the effort. William Landis comes to mind in terms of succeeding. I've been

fortunate to have known quite a few famous people and that makes me work harder to reach my goals even in my old age. Being nominated for the Rhysling and Dwarf Stars, and seeing my works in Pinterest also inspire me when I am down.

Whose poetry has influenced you the most?
I'd say that Edgar Allen Poe, Langston Hughes, and Lenard D Moore's poetry have influenced me the most. Poe's work puts the dread in you. I like Hughes' humor. Moore puts some "soul" into his work.

Did you begin writing haiku before you branched out to scifaiku?
Yes. I wrote haiku first. While teaching adult education classes in Detroit in the late Seventies I came upon a book that had haiku in it. When I read a book review of Lenard Moore's The Open Eye, I got deeply interested in haiku. I ordered The Red Pagoda edited by Lewis Sanders and was hooked by all the beautiful haiku in it.

How did you learn about scifaiku?
It was perhaps through the online Yahoo science fiction poetry group around two thousand-three. learned more about the genre in Starsong and Scavenger's Newsletter. Just as haiku puts you in the writer's "moment"; horror and science fiction ku can place the reader in that moment. Scary!

What poetry mags do you read/contribute to?
I read and contribute to Scifaikuest, Illumen, Star*Line, Cattails, and Haibun Today. Other magazines that include poetry are The Fifth Di..., Valley Voices, Spaceports & Spidersilk, The Martian Wave, Tales from the Moonlit Path, and Space & Time.

from the depths,
    the creature's yearning
      for a cigarette
        boat ~
      blown out of
      the water,
taking a smokeless pow~
der

Arey

FAVORITE POEM
by editor t. santitoro

genship gardening
telling tales of suns and fields
to shoots in a cup

David C. Kopaska-Merkel

The longing in this poem is SOOOO palpable; the wistfulness so tangible! WELL DONE!-t.santitoro, editor

www.ingramcontent.com/pod-product-compliance
Lightning Source LLC
LaVergne TN
LVHW092059060526
838201LV00047B/1461